"The Canadians . . . were marked out as storm troops. Whenever the enemy found the Canadian Corps coming into the line they prepared for the worst."

— British Prime Minister David Lloyd George

FROM VIMY TO VICTORY

CANADA'S FIGHT TO THE FINISH IN WORLD WAR I

HUGH BREWSTER

SCHOLASTIC CANADA LTD.

IT WAS A QUIET NIGHT ON VIMY RIDGE

with no sniper fire and no enemy shells crashing down. But Will Bird was miserable nonetheless. After a long, cold day of stringing barbed wire and digging trenches, he had nowhere to sleep. Then a low voice called out to him in the darkness. Will crept toward it and found two soldiers lying in a bivouac they had dug in an old railway

embankment. They invited Will into their "bivvy" and he quickly crawled under the groundsheet pegged over it. He was asleep in seconds and the next thing he knew, the groundsheet had been yanked away and a firm hand was pulling him upward.

"Get your gear," his brother Steve said.

Will was very surprised to see him. "Why didn't you write Mother?" he asked Steve groggily.

"Wait! Don't talk yet," his brother replied as he gestured for him to follow. Will struggled to keep up with Steve as he stumbled behind him in the dawn light.

Soon they were in some bombed-out ruins. Steve disappeared around a corner and Will followed, but couldn't find him. "Steve!" he called out. Then he remembered that his brother had been killed in battle two years before. Will couldn't believe he had lost him again. Sinking down on his kit bag, he fell into an exhausted sleep. Before long, someone was shaking him awake.

"He's here!" his friend Tommy shouted.

"What's all the fuss about?" Will asked.

"Don't you know a big shell landed in that bivvy?" Tommy replied. "They've been digging around it. All they've found is Jim's helmet and one of Bob's legs."

Will's sergeant and then an officer arrived. "What made you leave that bivvy?" they asked.

Will then described how the ghost of his brother had saved his life.

When he had finished, the officer said quietly, "You have had a wonderful experience."

(Right) A painting by Paul Nash captures the atmosphere of the trenches at night. (Above) Will Bird was a 25-year-old private from Amherst, Nova Scotia, who was in the Black Watch Regiment of Canada. His brother Stephen had died in 1915. "If I don't come back," he had once told Will, "maybe I'll find a way to come and whisper in your ear."

"As the guns spoke, over the [sand]bags they went — men of Cape Breton, sons of Nova Scotia and New Brunswick, French Canadians and Westerners — all Canucks. . . . It was the most spectacular victory. . . . and Canada may well be proud of the achievement." — Sergeant Percy Willmot

At dawn on April 9, 1917, the Canadians climbed out of their trenches (left) and began advancing through the enemy barbed wire (below). Within a few hours they had reached the crest of Vimy Ridge (opposite).

OVER THE TOP AT VIMY RIDGE

The guns began booming before dawn on Monday, April 9, 1917, signalling the start of the attack on Vimy Ridge. For months, all four divisions of the Canadian Corps had been preparing for this day. But Will Bird would not be a part of it. A severe case of mumps had put him in a hospital tent behind the lines. He really wished that he could be with his platoon — yet getting the mumps likely saved his life. Of the 722 men from his unit, the 42nd Battalion of the 3rd Division, 302 would be either killed or wounded in the assault on this feared enemy bastion.

Despite heavy casualties, the many weeks of careful planning paid off. By noon on that Easter Monday, most of Vimy Ridge was in Canadian hands. After some ferocious fighting, the highest point on the ridge, Hill 145, was taken that evening, and the woods below it early the next morning. Two days later on another hill called "the Pimple," the last German stronghold was seized.

From the blackened and blasted heights of the ridge, the Canadians looked out over the peaceful Douai Plain dotted with stone farmhouses and trees that were just turning green. On the horizon they could see what looked like huge, black pyramids — the slag heaps outside the coal-mining town of Lens. None of them knew that there they would face another bloody encounter with the enemy.

"'Mid the War's great curse, Stands the Red Cross Nurse,
She's the rose of 'No Man's Land.'"

(Left) Sheet music for a popular song about war nurses. (Above) At a first-aid post, a nurse holds a dog given to her by a group of soldiers. (Opposite) Two nurses care for a wounded soldier who is being sent by train to a hospital in England.

A COSTLY VICTORY

Against impossible odds at Vimy Ridge, the Canadians had achieved the greatest victory on the Western Front — taking more ground, more prisoners and more guns than in any other Allied attack to date. It won great praise for the Canadian Corps and would soon be hailed as the victory that made Canada a nation. But it had come at heavy cost. In four days of fighting, 3,598 men had been killed and 7,004 wounded. April 9, 1917, still stands as the bloodiest day in our military history. Will Bird hardly recognized his platoon when he returned from hospital, since so many of his friends had been killed or wounded on the ridge.

"The casualties have simply filled all the hospitals hereabouts to overflowing," Nurse Clare Gass from Shubenacadie, Nova Scotia, wrote in her diary on April 15, 1917. She noted that many of the wounds were "heart-breaking" and that some of her patients were dying from poison gas. Clare was one of 2,800 nursing sisters, as they were known, who served in the Canadian Army Medical Corps, often in front-line field hospitals. Fifty-three Canadian nurses would die in the line of duty during the war.

"AN ODD SORT OF BLOKE"

"You cut that out!" Grace Macpherson (above) demanded. "Nobody's riding in my ambulance moaning like that!" Grace had been working round the clock taking wounded soldiers from Vimy Ridge to the hospital at Étaples. And she knew that expressing sympathy only made them — and her — feel worse. Sometimes her passengers would say, "You're an odd sort of bloke," since they could hardly believe that a woman was behind the wheel.

Grace had been only 22 when she announced to her family in Vancouver that she was going to France to "do her bit" for the war effort. She took a ship to London in August of 1916, and went to Canadian headquarters to offer her services. There, officials told her that the Western Front was no place for a woman. "I'll get there with or without your help," she replied. A few months later, she learned that women were being accepted as ambulance drivers, since men were needed at the Front. After arriving in France, she quickly learned how to tune an engine and fix flat tires, as well as carry stretchers and apply first aid. When Étaples was bombed in 1918, she filled her ambulance with the wounded, took them to the hospital and went back for more. One man called Grace Macpherson "the bravest of them all."

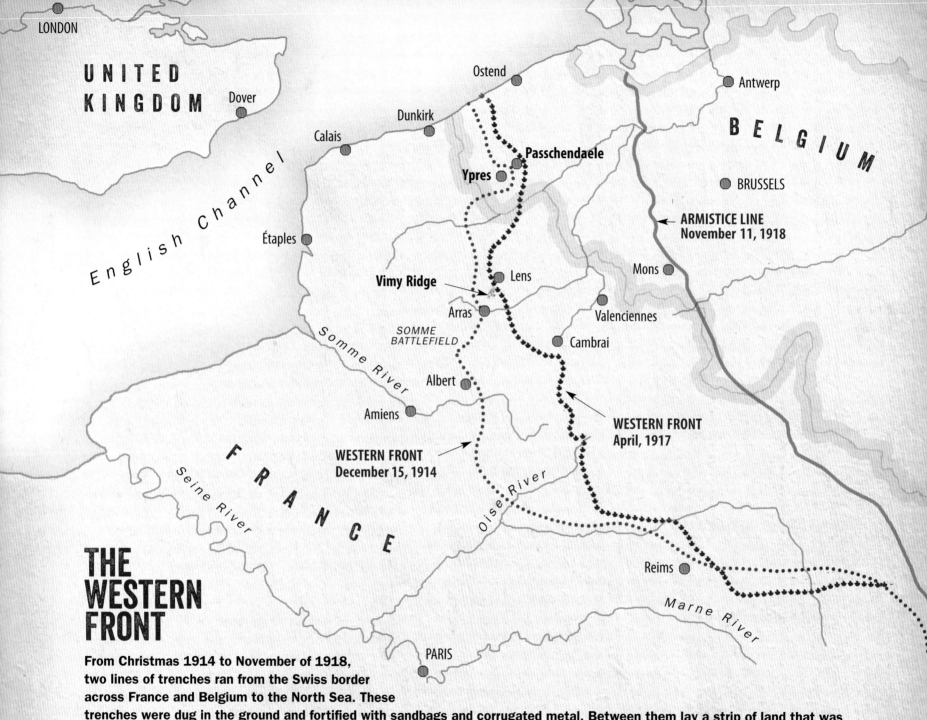

LONDON

UNITED
KINGDOM

Dover

Ostend

Antwerp

Dunkirk

B E L G I U M

Calais

Passchendaele

Ypres

BRUSSELS

English Channel

ARMISTICE LINE
November 11, 1918

Étaples

Lens

Mons

Vimy Ridge

Arras

Valenciennes

Somme River

SOMME
BATTLEFIELD

Cambrai

Albert

Seine River

F R A N C E

Amiens

WESTERN FRONT
April, 1917

WESTERN FRONT
December 15, 1914

Oise River

Reims

THE WESTERN FRONT

Marne River

PARIS

From Christmas 1914 to November of 1918,
two lines of trenches ran from the Swiss border
across France and Belgium to the North Sea. These
trenches were dug in the ground and fortified with sandbags and corrugated metal. Between them lay a strip of land that was
anywhere from 12 to 30 metres (though sometimes several hundred metres) wide, called No Man's Land. As one soldier from
Alberta wrote in 1917, "There is not a square yard of No Man's Land which is not saturated with the blood of either friend or foe."

A CANADIAN IN COMMAND

"No-one realizes better than I do the hard task that lies before me . . . " wrote Lt-General Arthur Currie in his diary in late June of 1917. At the age of forty-one, Currie had been given command of all four Canadian divisions. For the first time, the 100,000 men of the Canadian Corps had a Canadian as their commander. His English predecessor, Lt-General Julian Byng, was given great credit for turning his "wild colonial boys" into the most effective fighting force on the Western Front. "Bungo" Byng was much loved by his soldiers. The portly Currie, by contrast, seemed stiff and aloof and was nicknamed "Guts and Gaiters."

(Top) A portrait of Sir Arthur Currie painted in 1919. (Bottom) Currie maps out a battle plan with his officers at the Front in 1917.

But Currie was popular with his officers, since he would ask their opinions during his careful planning of battles and operations. And they respected the fact that he always tried to avoid needless loss of life. Officers observed that Currie would rather spend artillery shells than men to achieve his goals. So when Currie was told in July to mount a frontal attack on the town of Lens, he was not happy about it. "If we are going to fight at all," he said, "let us fight for something worth having."

HILL 70: THE HARDEST BATTLE

Arthur Currie knew that a direct assault on Lens would be murderous. In the ruins of the town the enemy would be waiting to ambush his men. He proposed instead that the Canadians take a hill to the north named Hill 70. Once they had captured this higher ground, the Germans would be forced to come out of Lens to counterattack and the Canadian gunners could fire down on them in what Currie called "an artillery killing ground."

As at Vimy four months before, the assault on Hill 70 began with a massive artillery bombardment in the darkness before dawn. Barrels of flaming oil were then hurled into the enemy lines to create a smokescreen. Once the big guns had pounded the barbed wire and enemy trenches, wave after wave of soldiers advanced over the low, scrubby chalk hill. Some had an easy stroll to their targets while others were caught in firefights or forced into brutal hand-to-hand combat with knives and bayonets. Those who made it to the crest of the hill faced the fiercest resistance of all from the enemy machine gunners below.

But Arthur Currie had prepared 250 machine-gun teams of his own. When the enemy's first counterattacks began at 8:15 that morning, the

More than 200 guns began firing at 4:25 a.m. on August 15, 1917, as 5,000 Canadians charged forward up Hill 70.

(Above, left) As the Canadians advanced through the smokescreen, gunfire from 300 Germans holed up in a chalk quarry slowed their progress. (Above, right) Some soldiers take cover in a captured enemy trench.

Canadians responded with a hail of gunfire. The Germans mounted attack after attack over the next three days and No Man's Land became carpeted with corpses. One stretcher-bearer exclaimed, "This isn't war — it's murder!" To force the enemy out of Lens, Currie's men lobbed lethal phosgene gas shells into the town. The Germans responded with mustard gas, a newer, deadlier gas that caused skin blisters, blindness and slow death. They also charged at the Canadians with flame-throwers — but were repelled nonetheless.

While rallying his men in one forward trench, a young officer from Quebec City named Okill Learmonth stood on the sandbags catching enemy grenades in his hands and tossing them back. Soon his body was so riddled with shrapnel that he eventually slumped to the floor of the trench, but he continued to give orders despite his many wounds. Eventually, two of his men carried him back for medical aid, but he insisted on stopping first to give a full report to his commanders. He died later that day and was posthumously awarded the Victoria Cross, the British Empire's highest award for gallantry.

Okill Learmonth

At dawn on August 18, Learmonth's men were among those who fought off the twenty-first and final German counterattack and the battle for Hill 70 was over. The Canadians had lost more than 5,000 men, but on the German side it was a bloodbath, with over 20,000 casualties. Arthur Currie called it "altogether the hardest battle in which the Corps had participated."

ATTACKING LENS

"Life in the underground defences of Lens is simply hell," one German prisoner told his Canadian captors. Yet despite the ceaseless pounding by artillery shells, the Germans stubbornly refused to retreat from the ruined town. Arthur Currie decided to force them out. He scheduled an attack on Lens to begin at 4:35 a.m. on August 21 — but just ten minutes beforehand, the Germans came charging forward with bayonets drawn. Then, as one Canadian soldier wrote, "A battle royal took place. After bombing and bayonet work we slowly forced the enemy back." In the outskirts of the town, however, more enemy soldiers lurked in cellars and alleyways. Grim house-to-house fighting followed. By the end of the day, the Canadians were forced to retreat, having lost 1,154 men.

With his forces tired and depleted, Arthur Currie should have realized that seizing Lens was impossible. But Major-General David Watson of the 4th Division persuaded him to allow his 44th Battalion, a unit from Manitoba, to mount another assault. At 3:00 a.m. on August 23, the Manitobans went in behind a creeping barrage. Some of them managed to clear out the enemy soldiers on a giant slag heap called the Fosse St. Louis, while a second group

"IMPORTANT MESSAGE!"

Private Harry Brown

As another German counterattack began on August 16, the men of the 10th Canadian Infantry Battalion desperately needed firepower from the artillery gunners in the rear. But the wires to their field telephones had been severed by enemy shellfire. A 19-year-old farm boy from Gananoque, Ontario, Harry Brown, volunteered with another ground runner to get the message back to company headquarters.

As the two young men tore off at top speed, enemy guns began firing at them. His companion was killed, but Harry ran on with one arm shattered. The bloodied young soldier finally reached the command post and fell into the arms of an officer. He managed to gasp out, "Important message!" before collapsing with the note in his hand. Harry Brown died the next day, but his actions saved the lives of hundreds of other Canadians. He was posthumously awarded the Victoria Cross, one of six Hill 70 soldiers to receive the medal, only two of whom would live to see it.

seized another mountain of coal waste known as the Green Crassier. Before long, however, the men of the 44th found themselves marooned on the heights with their ammunition running low. By the end of August 24, the Green Crassier had been lost and the survivors from the Fosse St. Louis were desperately trying to escape. This second assault had cost 258 casualties, yet Lens still remained in enemy hands. Arthur Currie decided to call it quits.

Despite the failure to capture Lens and the loss of 9,198 men killed or wounded, the operation at Hill 70/Lens was considered another Canadian victory. The Germans had been forced to divert troops to Lens from the fierce fighting farther north at Passchendaele, near Ypres, in Belgium — something that pleased the British commanders. Soon they would want the Canadians to join them in that deadly place.

(Above) Shelling had reduced the town of Lens to ruins.
(Below) German *flammenwerfers* could shoot flames up to 20 metres long.

A TOWN CALLED WIPERS

"You heard nothing but the steady tramp, tramp, tramp on the road," wrote Will Bird of the thousands of men marching north toward Ypres in early October 1917. None of them were happy about going there. Will's friends cursed the place they called "Wipers" and knew that it was a likely place to get wiped out. Arthur Currie didn't want to go to the Ypres Salient either. He knew that thousands of British and Australian soldiers had already perished there trying to take Passchendaele Ridge. "Let the Germans have it!" Currie raged to his staff. "Let them rot in the mud! It isn't worth a drop of blood!" He told the British commander-in-chief, Field-Marshal Sir Douglas Haig, that he would lose 16,000 Canadians if they had to fight there.

"Passchendaele must be taken," Haig replied firmly. "Some day I will tell you why."

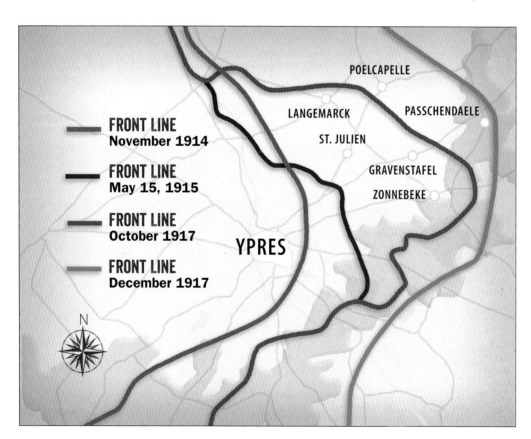

FRONT LINE
November 1914

FRONT LINE
May 15, 1915

FRONT LINE
October 1917

FRONT LINE
December 1917

POELCAPELLE

LANGEMARCK

ST. JULIEN

PASSCHENDAELE

GRAVENSTAFEL

ZONNEBEKE

YPRES

N

THE YPRES SALIENT

A U-shaped bulge in the trench lines in Flanders was known as the Ypres Salient. It was the scene of intensive fighting throughout the war, since losing it would allow the enemy to seize vital ports on the English Channel. In November of 1914, Allied forces had prevented the Germans from taking Ypres, though it had cost them over 100,000 casualties. In April of 1915, more than 6,000 Canadians had been killed or wounded at the 2nd Battle of Ypres, where they had faced the first-ever use of poison gas. A British offensive against Passchendaele Ridge, known as the 3rd Battle of Ypres, began on July 31, 1917, but by mid-October most of the advances made had been lost. The dispirited British then turned to the Canadians for help.

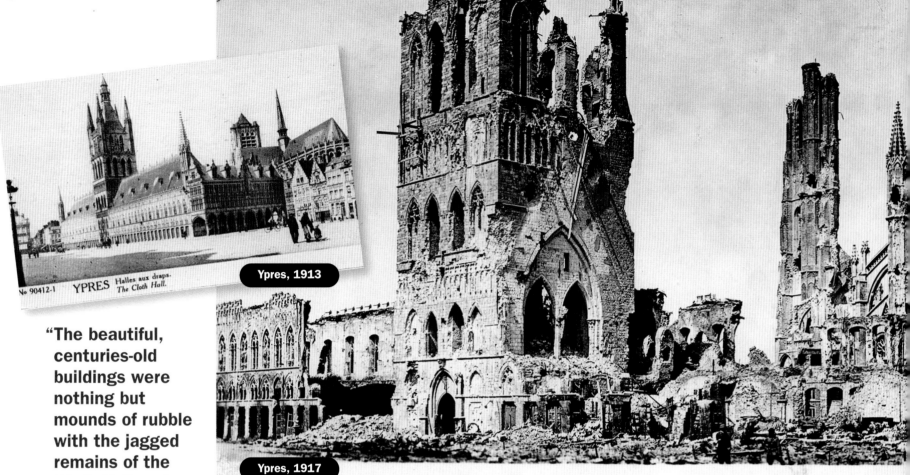

Ypres, 1913

YPRES Halles aux draps. The Cloth Hall. No 90412-1

Ypres, 1917

"The beautiful, centuries-old buildings were nothing but mounds of rubble with the jagged remains of the Cloth Hall and cathedral towers standing out as stark monuments to the destructive powers of modern war."

— Lt-Colonel Agar Adamson, Princess Patricia's Canadian Light Infantry

Field-Marshal Sir Douglas Haig (at right) had staked his career on making a breakthrough in the Ypres Salient. His plan was to take Passchendaele Ridge and then sweep north to capture key German submarine bases on the Belgian coast. He thought this might even break the enemy's resolve and win the war. Lt-General Arthur Currie (at left) could not defy Haig's orders to bring the Canadians to Ypres, but he could wring some concessions from him. Currie flatly refused to report to General William Gough, the British commander who had failed in the Passchendaele offensive. Currie also demanded time to make plans in the same careful way that had won victory at Vimy.

"Thirty men tried to pull a gun ... The mud gripped the wheels like glue ... Often we sank in ... until the slime rose above our hips. The only thing solid underneath was a huddled dead man, and we stumbled over five or six during the morning." — Will Bird

DOING BATTLE IN A SEA OF MUD

Arthur Currie was shocked by the desolate quagmire of the Passchendaele battlefield. The bombing of creeks and drainage ditches had turned the area into a moonscape of mud pocked by craters of filthy water. The stench of death was everywhere. Currie immediately set to work. He wanted to build plank roads through the muck in the style of the corduroy roads of the Ontario pioneers. The British pooh-poohed this idea and said that no planks were available. Currie got permission to cut trees in a forest and set up a sawmill where his men made their own planks. Canadian engineers soon built duckboard paths through the mud and even constructed a light railway for hauling men and supplies. In only eight days, order had begun to emerge from chaos.

By October 23, Currie was ready to present his battle plans to Field-Marshal Haig. He proposed that Passchendaele Ridge would be taken in four attacks: the 3rd and 4th Divisions would advance on October 26 and 30 to clear the way for the capture of the ridge by the 1st and 2nd Divisions on November 6 and 10. Haig was very pleased with this plan, but Currie made him promise that the Canadians could leave as soon as Passchendaele was taken. "Canada is prepared to lose her sons in a big offensive," he said, "but won't stand for their lives to be frittered away."

(Opposite) War artist Alfred Bastien painted Canadian gunners trying to move a large artillery piece through the mud at Passchendaele. (Below, left) Soldiers use duckboards to make a path through the mire. (Below, right) A light railway moves supplies to the Front.

DEADLY PILLBOXES

The noise from the artillery bombardment that launched the Canadian offensive early on October 26 was so intense that one soldier claimed, "It made me feel as if my chest was being ripped open." As the men of the 3rd and 4th Divisions climbed out of their shell holes in the misty dawn light, the German artillery opened fire. Most of the shells landed in the mud, throwing up geysers of muck. Far deadlier was the machine-gun fire that spat from concrete "pillbox" fortifications that the Germans had built in a checkerboard pattern across the battlefield.

As the men of the 3rd Division advanced up the Bellevue Spur, fierce gunfire from pillboxes cut them down, forcing a retreat. But a platoon of the Cameron Highlanders of Winnipeg clung to their newly won positions, keeping the enemy at bay with their machine guns. Realizing that his men would soon be surrounded, Lieutenant Robert Shankland of the Camerons weaved his way back through the mud to bring up reinforcements. Captain Christopher O'Kelly of the 52nd Battalion, another Winnipegger, was ordered to go to Shankland's aid. As he and his men advanced up the spur, they spotted enemy soldiers heading toward the Camerons. O'Kelly's group attacked and routed the Germans, then destroyed six pillboxes that were blocking the advance. By that night they had seized 21 machine guns and taken 284 prisoners. Both O'Kelly and Shankland were awarded the Victoria Cross for their actions.

Despite this heroism, the 3rd Division managed to advance only a few hundred metres up Bellevue Spur that day. Farther south, the 4th Division moved the front line almost a kilometre closer to Passchendaele. Field-Marshal Haig telegraphed Currie to say that his men's performance was "remarkably fine." Yet to gain less than a kilometre of muddy ground, 2,871 Canadians had been either killed or wounded.

FRONT LINE October 15
FRONT LINE October 26
FRONT LINE October 30
FRONT LINE November 6
FRONT LINE November 30
FLOODED AREAS
SWAMPY AREAS
PILLBOXES
HIGHER GROUND

BRITISH FORCES
VAPOUR FARM
BELLEVUE SPUR
GERMAN FORCES
PASSCHENDAELE
CANADIAN FORCES
CREST FARM
GRAVENSTAFEL RIDGE
PASSCHENDAELE RIDGE
AUSTRALIAN/NEW ZEALAND FORCES

Because of the flooded battlefield, Arthur Currie had to divide his forces into two. On October 26 the 3rd Division would advance up a knoll called the Bellevue Spur, while the 4th Division moved up Passchendaele Ridge.

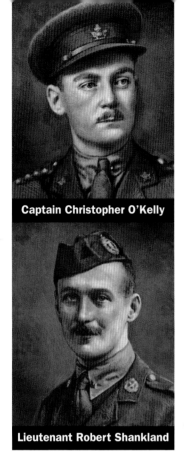

Captain Christopher O'Kelly

Lieutenant Robert Shankland

"SHEER, UNADULTERATED BRAVERY"

Private Tommy Holmes

Gunfire from a German pillbox supported by two machine-gun nests sent the men of the 4th Canadian Mounted Rifles diving for cover on October 26. "Our boys were going down pretty fast when I took it into my head that it was high time to shut [the guns] up," recalled Private Tommy Holmes, a feisty nineteen-year-old from Owen Sound, Ontario. With a grenade in each hand, Tommy ran toward the machine guns as bullets tore up the ground around him. Sliding into a shell hole, he waited while the German gunners reloaded and then crawled forward and lobbed his two grenades with such precision that he blew up both machine guns. After racing back for more grenades, he charged toward the pillbox. Dashing around behind it, he threw a grenade into the rear gun slit. A loud explosion erupted, then nineteen Germans — lucky enough to have survived the blast — came out with their hands up. One of Tommy's platoon mates said, "As an example of sheer, unadulterated bravery, it could hardly be surpassed." Tommy Holmes had the Victoria Cross pinned to his chest by King George V, becoming one of the youngest Canadians ever to receive the coveted medal.

THE BLOODY SECOND
ASSAULT

For the second attack on October 30, Arthur Currie's goal was to move his troops a thousand metres closer to the outskirts of Passchendaele. As the big guns began firing at 5:50 a.m, Major George Pearkes signalled to the men of the 5th Canadian Mounted Rifles to follow him out of their trenches. Suddenly Pearkes was knocked to the ground. Shrapnel had pierced his left thigh. "Now, I've got it," he thought.

Several of his men urged him to go back for medical aid, but Pearkes, a former Mountie from Alberta, said to himself, "I've got to go on . . . wounded or not." He struggled to his feet and limped forward as his men fell in behind him. Their orders were to capture Vapour Farm on the attack's left flank. Through withering gunfire and shelling, a bleeding Pearkes led his men over several hundred metres of muddy ground.

On reaching Vapour Farm, they charged with bayonets drawn and overpowered the enemy machine guns hidden in the haystacks of the ruined farmyard. Pearkes's men were now farther forward than any other Canadian force, but the Rifles were down to fewer than 40 men and in danger of being surrounded, cut off and

Major George Pearkes

(Opposite) Canadian soldiers crouch in Passchendaele shell holes. (Below) Two soldiers in a trench send a carrier pigeon skyward to carry a message back to headquarters.

destroyed. He attached a *Need Reinforcements* note to a carrier pigeon and sent it flying back to headquarters. His men took cover in a series of shell holes and managed to hold off enemy attacks until help arrived later that night. "Our men cannot be beaten," Pearkes wrote in a letter to his mother from a field hospital. Major Pearkes was awarded the Victoria Cross for leading one of the bravest small-group actions of the war. "I would have followed him through Hell if I had to," said one of his soldiers.

By the night of October 30 the Canadians almost had Passchendaele within their grasp. The 3rd Division was on drier ground on Bellevue Spur and, farther south, the 85th Highlanders from Nova Scotia had battled to the outskirts of Passchendaele, while the 72nd Battalion from Vancouver had swept the Germans from Crest Farm, only a hundred metres outside the village. But 1,429 men had been wounded that day and 884 killed — one man sacrificed for every metre of ground gained.

HUGHIE, THIS IS SUICIDE."

People said that Talbot Papineau would be Canada's prime minister one day. A gifted speaker and writer, the 34-year-old officer was also handsome, charming and athletic. A grandson of Louis-Joseph Papineau, the leader of the 1837 Lower Canada Rebellion, Talbot had grown up at Montebello, the family's country estate, where he spoke English with his American mother and French with his father. He attended McGill University and then won a Rhodes Scholarship to Oxford. When war broke out in 1914, he enlisted in Princess Patricia's Canadian Light Infantry and won the Military Cross for bravery in February of 1915. Later that year he was sent to hospital with acute battle fatigue and in 1916 was given a staff job behind the lines.

While working at Canadian headquarters in France, he wrote an open letter to his cousin, Henri Bourassa, a prominent spokesman against the war. In it, Papineau said that French and English Canadians dying together in the war could "cement a foundation for a true Canadian nation." When published, this letter and Bourassa's reply made Talbot Papineau famous. But by 1917 he was beginning to feel guilty that he was not in the front lines. He rejoined his regiment and on October 30 prepared to lead his men out of the trenches at Passchendaele.

When the enemy barrage began at 6:00 a.m., Papineau turned to Major Hugh Niven and said, "You know, Hughie, this is suicide." A moment later he was cut in two by an artillery shell. Papineau's severed legs were later seen sticking out of the mud, but his body was never recovered. His name inscribed on the Menin Gate (above) in Ypres is his only memorial. Yet his too-brief life stands as a symbol for all that Canada lost in the "war to end all wars."

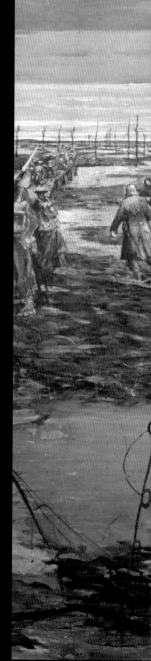

I died in hell — / (They called it Passchendaele). My wound was slight, / And I was hobbling back; and then a shell / Burst slick upon the duckboards; so I fell / Into the bottomless mud, and lost the light.

— from "Memorial Tablet," a poem by Siegfried Sassoon, 1918

(Right) Passchendaele as depicted by artist C.R.W. Nevinson

THE FINAL PUSH

The Germans sent reinforcements to defend to the death the rubble that had once been Passchendaele village. Arthur Currie also brought in fresh troops from the 1st and 2nd Divisions as well as men from Will Bird's 42nd Battalion. On the night of November 2, Will and 25 others were ordered out on a night raid to seize a pillbox. "The whole affair was cock-eyed," Will later wrote. "None knew the terrain. The place after dark was a swampy wilderness." Will was eventually knocked unconscious by an enemy shell and when he came to, his friend Mickey McGillivary was lying on top of him, covered in mud. But they were among the few lucky survivors.

Things went better when the third Passchendaele assault began on the morning of November 6. "The Canadians attacked so suddenly that we had no opportunity to use our guns," one German prisoner told his captors. Within three hours, most of the ridge that had cost so many lives was in Canadian hands. On November 10 the fourth assault faltered when British soldiers on the far left flank retreated in what Currie called "a panic." This left the men of the 10th Battalion from Calgary surrounded by hostile fire on three sides. "If the Canadians can hold on they are wonderful troops," an Australian soldier noted.

The Calgarians did hold on and by nightfall the front

(Opposite) Passchendaele Ridge after it had been taken by the Canadians. (Above, left) Two soldiers stand on a half-submerged rounded pillbox. (Above, centre) German prisoners help carry a stretcher along a light-rail line. (Above, right) Another German prisoner helps a Canadian soldier bury a lost comrade. (Below) Artist Fortunino Matania called this painting *The Last Message*.

line was secure. Within a few days the Germans retreated and the struggle for Passchendaele was over. Field-Marshal Haig had his victory and his job was saved, but Arthur Currie wrote to Prime Minister Robert Borden that it was "by no means worth the cost." Canadian casualties amounted to 15,654 — just shy of the 16,000 Currie had predicted. British and Commonwealth casualties in the battle for Passchendaele numbered 275,000, while German losses were 220,000. Five-and-a-half months later, the Germans would overrun Passchendaele Ridge.

Winston Churchill called the battle for Passchendaele a "forlorn expenditure of valour and life without equal in futility." For the men who had fought there, it was hell on earth. Will Bird would write, "[E]very man who had endured Passchendaele would never be the same again, was more or less a stranger to himself."

"I'M THROUGH. TELL MY MOTHER."

After the capture of Passchendaele village, German shells rained down on the Canadians. "There came a series of 'whizz-bangs,'" Will Bird remembered. "As the last soul-tearing smash crashed in my ears I saw Mickey spin and fall. I let go of Hughes and jumped to him. He had been hit in several places and could not live ten minutes. 'Mickey, Mickey!' I called his name and raised him up and he nestled to me like a child. 'I'm through,' he said. 'I don't want to kill people anyway. Tell my mother.' His voice was so low I could not hear, but his lips still moved. Little, white-faced Mickey. I held him in my arms until he stiffened, then laid him by the roadside . . . "

THE THOUSAND-YARD STARE

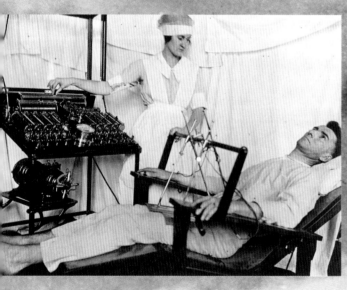

(Right) The fixed stare of this German soldier was a symptom of shell shock. More than 15,000 Canadians were diagnosed with this condition. (Above) A nurse administers electric shocks to a patient suffering from battle trauma.

During a shattering Passchendaele

bombardment, a man was blown into Will Bird's shell hole. As he pulled this soldier up out of the mud, Will saw that he "shook as with [fever], making animal noises." Another man's face, he noted, "had become like dough. His mouth dribbled. I could not look at him."

Given the horrors that Will and his fellow soldiers experienced, it is not surprising that some of them were afflicted with what we might now call PTSD (Post-Traumatic Stress Disorder). Yet a century ago, no one knew what this condition was. Early in the war, officers had observed that, after a battle, men might twitch or shake uncontrollably, have no memory, seem deaf or mute, or gaze off into the distance in what would come to be known as "the thousand-yard stare." At first it was thought that the deafening noise of artillery shells could stun the brain, and so this condition was called "shell shock." Good officers made sure that men showing symptoms of shell shock were sent to rest camps or hospitals, but others thought that these men were simply being fearful and "unmanly." One Canadian army doctor wrote that "shell shock is a manifestation of childishness and femininity." Such medical experts sometimes recommended that traumatized soldiers be treated with brutal electric shocks to get them back into service as quickly as possible.

A few desperate soldiers would resort to self-inflicted injuries to get out of the trenches. Others would hope for "a good Blighty" — a wound that wasn't too serious but required a hospital stay in England (nicknamed Blighty). Some were driven to become deserters — and this could bring on the harshest punishment of all.

"It was just daylight. A drizzling rain was falling. . . . The prisoner was seated on the box and his hands were tied behind the post. A round piece of white paper was pinned over his heart by the doctor as a guide for the men's aim." — Canon Frederick Scott

SHOT AT DAWN

Army chaplain Frederick Scott had been asked to give holy communion to a man condemned to be shot by firing squad at dawn on October 18, 1917. He was William Alexander, 37, from Calgary, who had served since September of 1914, and been promoted to a company quartermaster sergeant. During the attack at Hill 70, however, Sergeant Alexander had fled from the battle and been found later in a nearby village. Canon Scott was much affected by meeting the condemned man and tried to persuade senior officers to spare his life. But they refused. "I have seen many ghastly sights in the war," Scott wrote, "but nothing ever brought home to me so deeply the hideous nature of war, as did that lonely death on the hillside in the early morning."

William Alexander was one of 25 Canadians executed during World War I — 22 for desertion, one for cowardice and two for murder. On December 11, 2001, the government of Canada made a formal apology to the families of the 23 men executed for desertion or cowardice and placed their names in Parliament Hill's *Books of Remembrance*.

Canon Frederick Scott

KEEPING UP MORALE

As they tramped away from the Ypres Salient under grey November skies, the mood of the Canadian soldiers was as glum as the weather. They were being hailed as the invincible storm troops of the British army, but they had seen their comrades blown to pieces in a futile battle for a bog. "The year 1917 has been a glorious year for the Canadian Corps," claimed Arthur Currie, yet many of his men did not share his enthusiasm. Some even blamed Currie for the slaughter, not knowing how hard he had worked to avoid casualties.

The Canadians were headed back to Vimy Ridge. Over the winter and spring of 1917–18, they would defend the Vimy/Lens/Arras sector of the Western Front. Currie brought in fresh soldiers and had new trenches dug and kilometres of barbed wire strung. He also built up the morale of his men by giving them rest, better food and some recreation. Sports days and baseball games boosted soldiers' spirits, but most popular of all were the concert parties put on by soldiers who could sing, dance or perform skits. One troupe of soldier-entertainers, called The Dumbells, became especially popular — and very famous after the war.

(Above) A baseball game between teams from two Canadian battalions.

6

THE DUMBELLS

Captain Merton Plunkett (1), from Orillia, Ontario, enjoyed leading army singalongs and was asked to organize a concert party for the 3rd Division in 1917. He put together a group of soldiers (2) that included his brother, Al, who could sing and act, and Ivor "Jack" Ayre, who had played the piano in silent-movie cinemas. Plunkett named the troupe (3) after the crossed dumbells that were the symbol of the 3rd Division.

"We need girls to have a show!" several of the soldiers said, but

8

LONDON COLISEUM

THE
3rd CANADIAN DIVISIONAL CONCERT PARTY

"THE DUMBELLS"

Under the Direction of Capt. M. W. PLUNKETT
(By kind Permission of Major-Gen. L. J. LIPSETT, C.M.G.)

The Members of the Party have Served an average of Sixteen Months in the Firing Line, and are at present on leave from the Front

since there were no women at the Front, two of the men volunteered to be female impersonators. At their first show in the summer of 1917, the audience went dead silent when Private Ross Hamilton appeared as Marjorie (4) in a homemade dress and a wig of frayed rope. But after he sang "Hello, My Dearie" in a convincing falsetto, the men erupted in cheers. Another soldier, Alan Murray, did a star turn as Marie of Montreal (5).

The Dumbells' first show was a hit; soon they were touring to other army camps (6). British actresses donated costumes for the female impersonators, and musicians from military bands helped out with the music. The audiences sang along to songs like "Oh! It's A Lovely War" and Jack Ayre's "Dumbell Rag," but most popular of all were the skits that made fun of army life. Ted Charters did a hilarious bit as a pompous preacher sermonizing about kit inspection: "For no man knoweth when kit inspection cometh. . . . " (7). The Dumbells were invited to appear in London in 1918 (8), where they performed for the king and queen. After the war, the troupe put on touring revues in theatres all across North America and created the first Canadian show to appear on Broadway (9).

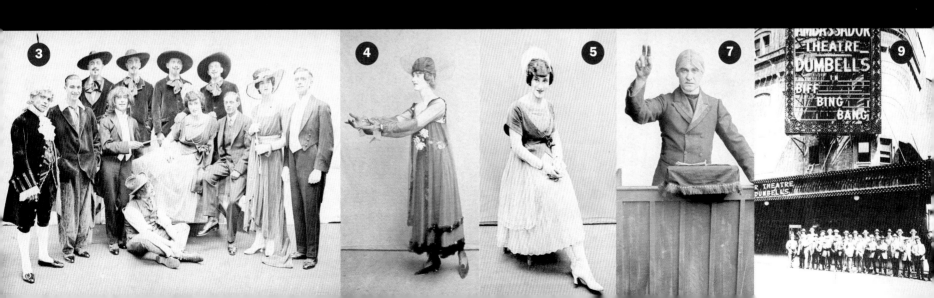

German emperor Kaiser Wilhelm II

> "We stand at the decisive moment of the world war and at one of the greatest moments in German history."
>
> — Kaiser Wilhelm II in a message to his troops before the March offensive

BREAKS THROUGH

"In March . . . everybody was jumpy," one Canadian soldier recalled. "Heinie was feeling out the strength of the different fronts . . . he'd send daylight raids across. . . ." That the Germans were planning a big offensive in the spring of 1918 was no secret. Their recent peace treaty with the new Bolshevik government that had seized power in Russia allowed them to move thousands of men from the Eastern to the Western Front. And with the United States now on the Allied side, it seemed likely that Germany would strike before most of the American troops could arrive in France. The big question was where exactly they would attack.

When the big German push came on March 21, 1918, it was not against the well-fortified Canadians but instead along a 90-kilometre section of the Front under the command of General William Gough, the same British commander that Currie thought had failed at Passchendaele. On the first day, the Germans smashed through the British defences and took 21,000 prisoners. By the third day, they had driven the British back 20 kilometres and were closing in on the city of Amiens and its main railway line to Paris. Germany's goal was to knock France out of the war, and it looked as if they might succeed. But what at first seemed a great victory would prove to be Germany's biggest blunder. After the Allies managed to stop their advance, the Germans found that they were unable to keep up with sending supplies and reinforcements to their overextended front lines. The Allies then began to push them back in what became known as the Hundred Days' Offensive — a series of battles in which Canadians would once again be the shock troops leading the advance.

THE GERMAN MARCH OFFENSIVE

Ypres
BRUSSELS
Vimy
Arras
Cambrai
Amiens
BELGIUM
GERMANY
GERMAN ADVANCES
Amiens-Paris Railway
FRANCE
PARIS

(Opposite) Canadian front-line spotters keep an eye out for enemy movements. (Right) A propaganda poster encourages German citizens to give "All for the Fatherland, All for Freedom."

GERMANY'S BLACK DAY

"Soldiers were on the move everywhere. The very air was tense," wrote Will Bird of the early days of August 1918. "We began moving without knowing where we were going. . . . [A]n order was pasted in every pay book. It read: KEEP YOUR MOUTH SHUT."

Arthur Currie was trying to do the near-impossible — move his 100,000 men and all their guns and equipment south to Amiens — in secret. To mislead the Germans, he dispatched two battalions and some medical units north to the Ypres Salient and had phony messages sent out describing an attack there. When Will Bird and the 42nd Battalion arrived near Amiens on the

night of August 6, they made camp with thousands of other men in a forest called Gentelles Wood, out of sight of German aircraft. On the roads, trucks and tanks moved through the darkness.

The goal of the attack was to push back the Germans and free the Amiens-Paris railway line. Canadian and Australian forces were to spearhead the assault, flanked by British and French troops along an 18-kilometre front. It was to be a new kind of battle, combining tanks, armoured cars and aircraft with cavalry and infantry. When the opening barrage began at 4:20 a.m. on August 8, army chaplain Frederick Scott wrote in his diary: "The noise was earth-shaking. I was so carried away by my feelings that I could not help shouting out,

(Opposite, top) A group of Canadian soldiers advances behind a party of French at Amiens. More than 400 tanks (opposite, bottom; and left) assisted the Amiens advance, though most were eventually knocked out by artillery shells, causing the men trapped inside to be burned alive. Armoured cars (right, upper and lower) could race down roads to fire at will with machine guns that could spit out 450 bullets per minute.

'Glory be to God for this barrage!' The German reply came, but, to our delight, it was feeble, and we knew we had taken them by surprise and the day was ours."

Through a heavy morning fog, the Canadians overran the first German positions. Corporal Herman Good, a burly lumberjack from Bathurst, New Brunswick, spotted three machine-gun nests in Harmon Wood and took them out single-handedly. Later, when his platoon was held up by a battery of field howitzers, Good took three of his men and charged with bayonets

Corporal Herman Good

drawn. They overpowered the gunners and took 28 prisoners. Corporal Good was later awarded the Victoria Cross.

By the end of the day, the Canadians had advanced 13 kilometres and taken 5,033 prisoners. To the German commander, General Erich Ludendorff, "August 8th was the black day of the German Army in the history of the war."

VICTORY BONDS WILL HELP STOP THIS —

KULTUR VS. HUMANITY.

AVENGE THE *LLANDOVERY CASTLE*!

On June 27, 1918, a Canadian hospital ship named the *Llandovery Castle* was torpedoed and sunk off Ireland by a German U-boat, with a loss of 234 lives. The U-boat crew also rammed and machine-gunned the survivors in lifeboats. Eighty-eight of the 94 Canadians on board died — including 14 Canadian nurses. In remembrance of this barbarous act, the Amiens attack was code-named L.C., and some Canadian officers told their men that *Llandovery Castle*! should be their battle cry.

"DON'T PUSH US ANY FURTHER."

Lieutenant Jean Brillant

The Germans were down but certainly not out at Amiens and the next day's fighting became much harder. Against fierce resistance the Canadians took the village of Le Quesnel on the morning of August 9 and pushed onward. Once again, a few brave men were willing to tackle the enemy single-handed. Near the village of Méharicourt, a young Québécois lieutenant named Jean Brillant raced forward and captured a machine gun that was firing on his 22nd Battalion. Although wounded, he refused treatment and soon led a charge in which 150 Germans and fifteen machine guns were captured. Brillant was wounded again, but then attacked a nearby field gun. He was wounded a third time, but still continued onward before collapsing from loss of blood. "I am through," he said to a junior officer in French. "Take charge of the company. I won't be here long." Brillant died two days later and was posthumously awarded the Victoria Cross.

The Canadians advanced another 6 kilometres on August 9, but 2,574 of them were killed or wounded. The following day, German reinforcements arrived and the fighting became desperate. After three more days of bloody conflict, the Allies' ammunition was running low and most of their tanks had been destroyed. "For God's sake, stop. Don't push us in any further. We'll get smashed," one soldier pleaded in his diary.

On August 13 Currie and the Australian commander told Sir Douglas Haig that the battle should be called off before their troops were "pounded to pieces." Haig reluctantly agreed, but immediately began planning another attack farther north. At Amiens the Canadians had lost 9,074 men, including extraordinary leaders like Jean Brillant. But it had been far worse for the Germans. After Amiens, even Kaiser Wilhelm had to admit, "We have reached the end of our capacity." Yet losing the war was unthinkable, so more hard warfare lay ahead.

A famous Canadian sniper, Henry Norwest, was killed at Amiens. Of Cree ancestry, Norwest was known among the enemy as a feared marksman. In trying to flush out a nest of German snipers on August 18, Norwest himself was killed by a sniper's bullet. He was one of 4,250 Métis and First Nations soldiers who served in the war.

(Above) Two cavalry soldiers escort German prisoners past Canadian infantrymen. At Amiens, fourteen German divisions were defeated by the Canadians and 9,311 prisoners taken. (Below) This Spandau 7.92-mm machine gun was one of over a thousand seized at Amiens.

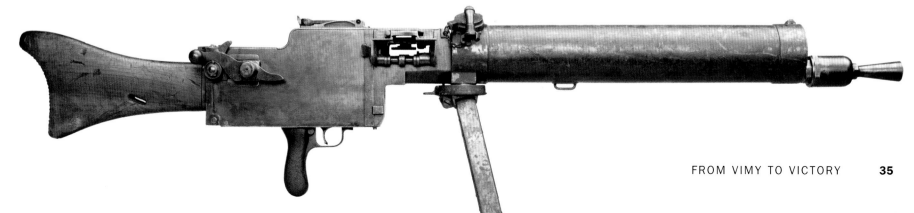

THE BATTERING RAM

"The Canadian Corps is really the battering ram with which we will break up the last line of resistance of the German army." — Marshal Ferdinand Foch, Allied Commander-in-Chief

From Amiens,

Will Bird and his battalion marched through the night to Arras, near Vimy. They thought they might get some rest there, but instead Will heard "a flood of rumours" about what might lie ahead " . . . and the pessimists . . . said we were in for it." The pessimists would prove to be right. Attacks were being planned for all along the Western Front and the Canadians had been selected to crack the enemy's most heavily fortified position, the dreaded Hindenburg Line. To reach it, they first had to run the gauntlet from Arras through a deadly obstacle course of trenches, pillboxes, gun batteries and fields of barbed wire, all defended by battle-hardened German troops. Arthur Currie was worried. He asked for a division of British soldiers to join his four Canadian divisions. And he decided to launch his attack in the middle of the night, rather than at dawn.

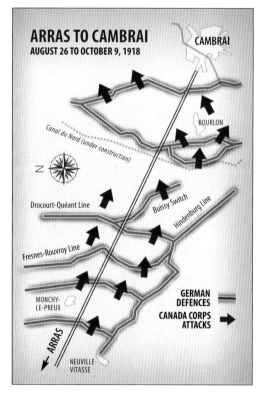

ARRAS TO CAMBRAI
AUGUST 26 TO OCTOBER 9, 1918

CAMBRAI

Canal du Nord (under construction)

BOURLON

Drocourt-Quéant Line

Buissy Switch

Hindenburg Line

Fresnes-Rouvroy Line

MONCHY-LE-PREUX

ARRAS

NEUVILLE-VITASSE

GERMAN DEFENCES ▬▬
CANADA CORPS ATTACKS ➤

At 3:00 a.m. on August 26, the Germans were taken by surprise; by 7:40 a.m. the Canadians had taken the town of Monchy. The going then got harder, but tanks helped crush the barbed wire that lay in their path. By evening they had advanced nearly 5 kilometres and taken 2,000 prisoners. The next day, as the Canadians pushed on toward the Fresnes-Rouvroy Line, the Germans attacked from the surrounding hills. Currie's men were badly hammered and it would take four more days, with heavy artillery and reinforcements being sent in, before the Fresnes-Rouvroy line was captured.

Now the near-impregnable Drocourt-Quéant Line lay ahead. Since this was "the backbone of his resistance," Currie wrote, "the Boche will fight very hard." The Germans moved in reinforcements to defend the D-Q Line, but on September 2 the Corps punched through and the 1st Division even went on to crush the Buissy Switch, the main defensive position beyond it. That night the enemy withdrew beyond the Canal du Nord. To Arthur Currie, the breaking of the D-Q Line was "one of the finest feats in our history." But it had cost him 11,423 men. And getting across the Canal du Nord would be his biggest challenge yet.

"The barbed wire was that thick . . . but our tanks . . . pushed it down and made a perfect bed for us to walk on. . . . And they had steel pillboxes and our tanks rolled right over the top of them."

— Private M.H. Timm, 21st Battalion

(Above) Canadians board trucks in Arras to head for the firing line.
(Below) They advance single file under German bombardment east of Arras.
(Right) Tanks provided useful support in the attack on the Drocourt-Quéant Line.

ACROSS THE VALLEY OF DEATH

"Old man, do you *really* think you can do it?" Julian Byng asked Arthur Currie. The British commanders had asked General Byng to talk some sense into Currie about his risky plan for taking the Canal du Nord. Since the canal itself was a nearly impassable barrier, Currie intended to attack farther south through an unfinished dry section of it. His troops could cross there and expand outward behind the German defences along the eastern shore of the canal. It was a complicated plan in which thousands of men had to be funnelled across a narrow opening where they could be cut down by enemy gunfire. Byng told Currie that if his plan failed, he would be fired and sent home. Currie replied that his men would "deliver the goods."

Yet as zero hour approached in the early morning of September 27, Currie grew more and more nervous. "Probably never in the war had we experienced a moment of deeper anxiety," wrote Canon Frederick Scott. "The men would have to climb down one side of the canal, rush across it, and climb up the other. Here, in mud and rain, weary and drenched to the skin, young Canadians were waiting to go through the valley of the shadow of death."

At 5:20 a.m. the early dawn was shattered by a deafening artillery barrage. Then the men of the 1st and 4th Divisions swarmed down and across the muddy canal bed and scrambled up the other side. They attacked the Germans before they could even man their defences, and took hundreds of prisoners. The 1st Division swung north to flush out the defenders along the bank while the 4th pushed on to clear the enemy from the heights of Bourlon Wood. And even while bullets flew, Canadian engineers began constructing a temporary bridge to span the canal.

The impregnable Hindenburg Line had been well and truly breached. The British generals who had been so skeptical sent Currie congratulations. Yet Currie knew that when the Germans were cornered they would fight back desperately — and very soon, they did.

(Above) Currie's former boss, Julian Byng (at left), quizzed him about his attack plan for the Canal du Nord. The banks of the canal (opposite, top, left) were well defended, so Currie decided to attack across a dry canal bed (opposite, bottom). (Opposite, top right) Canadian engineers began building a bridge spanning the canal right after the opening barrage.

LIBERATORS

When the Canadians entered Cambrai on October 9, they found the city ablaze. "This beautiful city has been willfully set on fire by the Boche," raged Arthur Currie. Some of his men tried to put out the flames while others chased the retreating Germans. With Cambrai taken, the Canadians soon felt their spirits rise. Currie could now see a chance for victory before the end of the year.

But the road to Cambrai had been bloody. After the Canal du Nord, the enemy had thrown everything they had against the Canadians. Since leaving Arras on August 26, the Corps had lost over 30,000 men: 4,367 killed, 24,509 wounded and 1,930 missing. As a soldier from one shattered battalion wrote, "Every time I look around for familiar faces, I find they have gone."

It helped that now the advancing Canadians were greeted as liberators. Will Bird wrote that the inhabitants of one French village were "almost delirious with joy" and that their children "ran alongside crying, 'Bon Canadaw!'"

The retreating Germans decided to make a stand at Valenciennes, a city near the Belgian border. They flooded most of the surrounding area by blasting canal dikes. The only dry approach to the city was blocked by a well-defended hill, Mont Houy. British commander General Horne decided that his men would take Mont Houy and the Canadians would then capture the city. On October 28 a Scottish division took Mont Houy, but couldn't hold it. Currie soon organized a devastating artillery barrage, and on November 1 his men overran Mont Houy and entered Valenciennes. The joyous citizens organized a welcoming ceremony, but General Horne insisted that British soldiers lead the parade with the Canadians bringing up the rear. Arthur Currie could barely contain his outrage.

(Opposite) Canadian soldiers enter a burning Cambrai and (above) later walk through a church destroyed by shelling. (Left) British general Henry Horne greets the mayor of Valenciennes, while Arthur Currie stands behind.

"Bird! Get your section ready at once.

Battle order!" snapped the company sergeant-major on the morning of November 10.

"What's up?" demanded Will Bird, now a sergeant.

"We're going to take Mons," the sergeant-major replied. "Get our men ready."

"Just a minute," said a soldier in Will's platoon. "The war's over tomorrow and everybody knows it. What kind of rot is this?"

"Watch what you say," the sergeant-major retorted. "Orders are orders. Get your gear on."

Will couldn't believe it. Only an hour before, the same sergeant-major had told him that an armistice would be signed the next day. Will had let out a loud whoop and broken into a war dance with Tom and Jim Mills, two brothers in his platoon. For days they had all sensed that the war was winding down. Since crossing into Belgium on November 6, they had seen Germans surrendering by the thousands. Will had spotted Belgian women chasing and beating German soldiers, taking revenge for four years of harsh occupation. In Germany itself, revolution was brewing. On November 9 Kaiser Wilhelm had been forced to flee across the border into exile in Holland. And in a train car in a forest in northern France, German representatives were negotiating the terms of surrender with Allied officials.

THE PURSUIT TO MONS

Kilted soldiers from Will Bird's 42nd Battalion on the advance. (Inset) A German sign points the way to Mons.

(Above, left) An enemy soldier surrenders and (above, right) two Canadians display a German flag captured from the Valenciennes city hall.

Yet the fighting continued. As Will lined up his men there was grumbling and cursing. One soldier said they should attack their own headquarters instead. Some accused their commander of being a glory seeker.

Arthur Currie did indeed want the glory of taking Mons. It was there that the British had suffered their first defeat of the war on August 23, 1914. Now the Canadians would have the honour of taking Mons back. But Currie hoped to do it without too many casualties.

That afternoon, as Will and his platoon advanced across an open field, German shells suddenly crashed

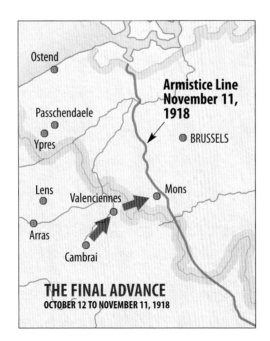

Ostend

Passchendaele

Ypres

**Armistice Line
November 11,
1918**

● BRUSSELS

Lens
Valenciennes

Mons

Arras

Cambrai

THE FINAL ADVANCE
OCTOBER 12 TO NOVEMBER 11, 1918

down near them. Will spied a brick building about the size of a garage. He and a few men dashed inside just as a huge shell exploded overhead. The force of it knocked Will to the ground.

"That was too close for comfort," he said as he scrambled up.

Behind him, Tom Mills cried out, "I'm hit!" Tom's brother, Jim, caught him as he sank to the ground.

"I saw he had a fearful wound in his stomach," Will later wrote. "He died as we looked at him."

Jim Mills went wild. He couldn't believe his brother was dead. And in less than twenty-four hours, the war would be over.

11TH MONTH, 11TH DAY, 11TH HOUR

At 6:30 a.m. on November 11, the first Canadians entered Mons. They roused the sleeping citizens by rattling their bayonets along the iron bars of cellar windows. It was then that Arthur Currie received word that all hostilities would cease at 11 a.m. "No shooting after eleven!" was the message passed on to the men.

As the clock ticked down to that hour, Private George Price from Moose Jaw, Saskatchewan, was sitting in a slit trench in a village outside Mons. When a Belgian woman waved at him from a nearby window, Price jumped up and ran to her, perhaps expecting a kiss. Instead, a sniper's bullet struck him in the chest and he died instantly at 10:58 a.m. — the last Canadian to be killed in the war.

Private George Price

(Above, left) Canadian pipers march through the streets of Mons on November 11, heading for the Grand Place, where more crowds waited. (Above, right) General Currie takes the salute on horseback as his men parade past that afternoon.

Only moments later, kilted Canadian bagpipers began leading a parade toward the main square in Mons, greeted by wild cheering and many hugs and kisses. Will Bird missed out on the celebration, as he was trying to keep Jim Mills out of trouble. The frenzied Mills was swearing that he was going to shoot Currie or whoever was responsible for his brother being killed for nothing. An officer told Will to get Mills so drunk he wouldn't remember anything. Will put Jim in the care of his friend Tommy, since he had to give a detailed report on the two men from his platoon who had been killed on the way to Mons. When he had finished, he fought his way through crowded streets until he found Tommy, who told him that Jim Mills was lying in a nearby cellar, as "drunk as a boiled owl."

Not long after this, an elderly couple called out,

"Canada!" and waved at Will from the door of their small cottage. They invited him in for a hearty meal of vegetable soup, bread and cheese.

Will was so exhausted that he fell asleep at the table. The old Belgian man helped him into bed and when he awoke it was dark outside. His hosts filled a tin bath for him and as he was dressing after bathing, he heard a noise from inside a large cupboard. Pulling open the door, he found a German soldier crouched among a pile of clothing. He looked about eighteen and was quivering with fear. Will pulled him up and took a long blue coat and cloth cap out of the cupboard. The young German put the civilian clothes on over his uniform and Will quietly escorted him to the front door.

"*Kamerad!*" the German said. He shook Will's hand and then slipped away into the night.

"THIS IS NOT PEACE."

"Nothing but home for us now!" a joyous soldier shouted to Will Bird in Mons on November 11. But it would be many months before the battle-weary Canadians were allowed to return home. The 1st and 2nd Divisions were ordered to Germany as part of an occupying force. Will Bird and his battalion returned to England and eventually sailed for Halifax in March. The last of the Canadians were not welcomed home until August of 1919.

When a young German soldier named Adolf Hitler heard the news of the armistice on November 11, he wept and vowed to avenge this shame on the Fatherland. In the Treaty of Versailles that formally ended the war on June 28, 1919, Germany was stripped of some of its territories and forced to pay heavy reparations to the victors. On reading the treaty, Marshal Foch, the supreme Allied commander, said, "This is not peace. It is an armistice for twenty years."

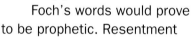
The Vimy Memorial

Foch's words would prove to be prophetic. Resentment over Germany's humiliation helped bring Adolf Hitler and his Nazi party to power in 1933. When Hitler's forces overran France in June of 1940, he made sure that the surrender was signed in the same train car in which Germany's defeat had been sealed in 1918. Hitler also took a victory lap around the Canadian war monument atop Vimy Ridge — though he did not destroy it, as some Canadians feared he might.

Today that gleaming white memorial still stands, paying moving tribute to the more than 66,000 Canadians who died in "the war to end all wars." A statue of a weeping woman looks out over the Douai Plain, symbolizing a young nation mourning her lost sons and daughters. It is a profoundly moving place to reflect on Canada's enormous sacrifice, the valour of our soldiers, and the horror of war.

The men of Will Bird's 42nd Battalion board SS *Adriatic* on their way home in March 1919.

GLOSSARY

artillery: the large guns that fired high-explosive shells that could also contain shrapnel, poison gas or smoke.

bivouac: an improvised shelter for soldiers, nicknamed a bivvy.

Boche: a derogatory name used for the German enemy. Also: Fritz, Heinie and Hun.

Bolshevik: the radical party led by Vladimir Lenin that seized power in Russia in 1917, and later formed the state known as the Soviet Union.

creeping barrage: a staged infantry advance behind a moving (or creeping) line of artillery fire.

duckboards: sections of wooden walkways put in the bottom of trenches.

Fritz, Heinie, Hun: see Boche.

infantry: soldiers trained to fight on foot.

Kamerad: German for "comrade" or "friend."

kit bag: a large canvas pack that could carry such items as a soldier's socks, greatcoat, water bottle or mess tin.

mustard gas: a poison gas with a brownish-yellow colour that could cause serious blisters on both skin and lungs, and could blind and kill.

phosgene gas: a lethal, colourless, poison gas with an odour like freshly-cut grass that caused its victims to cough and choke.

pillbox: a concrete fortification with holes through which guns could be fired.

platoon: the smallest military unit with 32 to 48 men plus officers. In the Canadian Corps, there were 4 platoons in a company and 4 companies in a battalion. A brigade had 4 battalions and a division had 3 brigades.

salient: a military position that projects into enemy territory.

shrapnel: metal fragments from exploding shells, and small shot that was contained in artillery shells.

slag heaps: large piles of coal waste left by coal mining.

sniper: a skilled shooter who could pick off enemy soldiers from a concealed location.

INDEX
Page numbers in italics refer to illustrations or maps

RECOMMENDED READING

For young readers

At Vimy Ridge: Canada's Greatest World War I Victory by Hugh Brewster (Scholastic). Companion volume to this book.

Passchendaele: Canada's Triumph and Tragedy on the Fields of Flanders by Norman Leach (Coteau Books).

Remembering John McCrae and *The Unknown Soldier* (Scholastic) by Linda Granfield, author of *Where Poppies Grow* (Fitzhenry & Whiteside).

The War to End All Wars by Jack Batten (Tundra), author of *Silent in an Evil Time: The Brave War of Edith Cavell* (Tundra).

Adult reading level

At the Sharp End and *Shock Troops* by Tim Cook (Penguin). Outstanding 2-volume history of Canada's role in World War I.

For King and Empire by Norm Christie (CEF Books). Excellent, detailed series of books and TV programs (available on YouTube) on Canadians in the Great War.

Ghosts Have Warm Hands by Will Bird (CEF Books). A gripping war memoir.

Sir Arthur Currie: A Biography by Daniel Dancocks (Methuen).

Vimy by Pierre Berton (Anchor) and *Victory at Vimy* by Ted Barris (Thomas Allen). Two good accounts of the famous battle.

Websites

The Canadian War Museum, **Library and Archives Canada**, **Veterans Affairs Canada** and the **Canadian Great War Project** all offer useful information about World War I.

ABOUT THE AUTHOR

Hugh Brewster is the author of four previous award-winning books about Canadians under fire. *On Juno Beach* received the Information Book Award in 2005 and *At Vimy Ridge* won the 2008 Norma Fleck Award for Canadian Children's Non-Fiction. In 2009 *Dieppe: Canada's Darkest Day of World War II* was described by the *Globe and Mail* as "simply superb" and his novel *I Am Canada: Prisoner of Dieppe* won the 2012 Hackmatack Award. He has also written or co-written ten other books for both children and adults and is a sought-after speaker in schools and libraries.

ACKNOWLEDGEMENTS

I'm grateful to historian Tim Cook for his expert review of the text and layouts and also for his superb books on World War I. Special thanks are due to: Gordon Sibley for his excellent design and map work; Tom Deacon for his great-uncle's letters and photos; Sharif Tarabay for his illustrations of soldiers; my partner Phillip Andres for help and photography during research on the Western Front; the archives and museums who have provided images; my patient editor at Scholastic Canada, Sandra Bogart Johnston.

PICTURE CREDITS

All maps and diagrams are by Gordon Sibley. All colour portraits of soldiers are by Sharif Tarabay.

Author's Collection: Jacket and p. 1 (badge); p. 2 (from *Ghosts Have Warm Hands*); p. 12 (right); p. 15 (top, left); p. 19 (top, right) and grenade; p. 22 (bottom); p. 27 (from *The Great War As I Knew It*); p. 29 (bottom, far right); p. 46 (right).
Bundesarchiv: p. 13 (bottom) Bild: 183-R05148; p. 26 (right) Bild: R22888.
Canadian War Museum: Paintings are from the Beaverbrook Collection of War Art. Front Jacket: *Over the Top: Neuville-Vitasse* by Alfred Bastien, CWM 19710261-0056; p. 7 (top, right) CWM/MCG photos 0.1469a; p. 9 (top) *Lieutenant General Sir Arthur Currie* by Sir William Orpen, CWM 19710261-0539; p. 13 (top) CWM 19780067; p. 16 *Canadian Gunners in the Mud, Passchendaele* by Alfred Bastien, CWM 19710261-0093; p. 35 (bottom) CWM 19880212-027; p. 42 (inset, top) CWM 19390001-927.
David M. Rubenstein Rare Book & Manuscript Library, Duke University: p. 6 (sheet music).
Electrotherapy Museum: p. 26 (left).
Imperial War Museum: p. 3 *Ypres Salient at Night* by Paul Nash, IWM ART 1145; pp. 22-23 *The Harvest of Battle* by C.R.W. Nevinson, IWM ART 1921; p. 25 (bottom, right) *The Last Message* by Fortunino Matania, IWM ART 5192.
Library and Archives Canada: All numbers are Mikan numbers. Front jacket (inset, soldiers) 3404743; Endpapers (front) 3522043, (back) 3404743; p. 4 (inset, bottom) 3404765;

p. 5 3192998; p. 7 (left) 3395847; p. 9 (bottom) 3404516; p. 10 3195150; p. 11 (top, right) 3395589; p. 15 (bottom) 3404878; p. 17 (bottom, left) 3522043; p. 20 3233069; p. 21 (bottom) 3380990; p. 22 (Papineau) 7902; p. 24 3329056; p. 25 (top, left) 3397881; p. 28 (top, left) 3384449, (top, right) 3522190, (bottom) 3667289; p. 29 (top, right) 3522922, (bottom, far left) 3194831, (2nd from left) 3522927, (3rd from left) 3522926, (2nd from right) 3522919; p. 30 3395600; p. 32 (top) 3643060, (bottom) 3395384; p. 33 (top, left) 3395390, (top, upper) 3522240, (right, lower) 3395367; p. 35 (top) 3239910; p. 37 (top) 3404834, (middle) 3404585, (bottom) 3194820; p. 38 3404870; p. 39 (top, left) 3329289, (top, right) 3194494, (bottom) 3329287; p. 40 (top) 3520999, (bottom) 3194945; p. 41 (top) 3403971, (bottom) 3397435; p. 42 (full image) 3355935; p. 43 (top, left) 3403198, (top, right) 3397966; p. 44 (top, left) 3522363, (top, right) 3522364; p. 45 (right) 3522365; p. 46 (left) 3522989; Back jacket (tank photo) 3404585, (poster) 2897699.
Library of Congress Prints and Photographic Archive: p. 31 (top, right), (bottom, poster); p. 33 (bottom, poster).
Tom Deacon Collection: p. 4 (full image); p. 6 (full image); p. 11 (top, left); p. 15 (top, right); p. 17 (right); p. 25 (top, centre and right).

Produced by Whitfield Editions
Designed by Gordon Sibley

www.scholastic.ca

Library and Archives Canada Cataloging in Publication

Brewster, Hugh, author
From Vimy to victory : Canada's fight to the finish in World War I / by Hugh Brewster.

ISBN 978-1-4431-2461-4 (bound)

1. World War, 1914-1918–Personal narratives, Canadian–Juvenile literature.
2. Currie, Arthur, Sir, 1875-1933–Diaries–Juvenile literature.
3. World War, 1914-1918–Canada–Juvenile literature.
4. Canada. Canadian Army–History–World War, 1914-1918–Juvenile literature. I. Title.

D640.A2B74 2014
j940.4'8171
C2013-907928-9

SCHOLASTIC CANADA LTD.
604 King Street West,
Toronto, Ontario, Canada
M5V 1E1

5 4 3 2 1   Printed in Malaysia 108   14 15 16 17 18